CANDLESTICK PATTERNS FOR BEGINNERS

The True Price Action Vol 1

Derby Tendai Matoma

Derby Tendai Matoma

CANDLESTICK PATTERNS FOR BEGINNERS

The True Price Action Series Vol 1

CONTENTS PAGE

Candlestick Patterns for Beginners
  Contents Page

Foreword

Chapter 1 What is a candlestick?
Chapter 2   Bullish continuation patterns
Chapter 3 Bearish Continuation Patterns
Chapter 4 Trend Reversal Candlestick Patterns
Chapter 5   How to trade with candlestick patterns

FOREWORD

If you have been trying to trade securities or do a simple technical analysis, you have encountered a strange data presentation that employs candlesticks. Most systems present data in line graphs, bar graphs, tables, and pie charts. These are very effective depending on the type of data being represented and how regular the data needs to be updated.

The story is different in financial markets as market data needs to be updated every second. Line graphs effectively show market prices; however, they don't give technical traders the privilege to analyze the market on a short time basis. Technical day traders need to analyze market movements at brief periods, some as low as a 1-minute time frame. As a result, they use the tool known as **candlesticks**. Conventionally traders regard candlesticks as market indicators. I prefer considering them as an effective form of data presentations, making it easy to analyze market movements at smaller time frames.

Munehisa Homa, a genius Japanese rice trader, introduced candlesticks to the world of trading in the 18th century. They were widely accepted in the western world after Steve Nison wrote about them in his candlesticks charting book; since then, technical analysis has been easy. I have no doubt that understanding candlesticks is pivotal for the success of technical analysts. However, most books on candlesticks make readers focus on candlesticks' names instead of the cause and effect. This is the primary reason I wrote this E-book. Over the years, I have seen people memorizing candlestick patterns when it all boils down to understanding the momentum in the market and how it manifests. More so, the examples people focus on are textbook pictures that do not give the novice a true reflection of market conditions. 70 % of learners experience a reality shock upon looking at real-life charts, only to realize textbook examples are different from real-life setups. This book will combat this challenge through real-life examples from my charts.

In this book, I will explain various candlestick patterns. I will focus on the logic of the movement exhibited and less focus on the nomenclature of the candlesticks patterns. What truly matters is the ability to interpret the market movement; naming the movement is how traders try to sound fancy. There is nothing fancy about naming candlestick patterns neither is there any credit to it. With that being said, don't push hard memorising names. Instead, try to understand the behaviour of market participants, which the candlestick patterns reflect.

Think of the market as a tug of war between buyers and sellers.

Whoever wins at a given moment gets rewarded with an opportunity to move the market and a particular moment. With buyers endeavouring to drive the market upward and sellers are pushing downwards. This specific school of thought brought up the familiar analogy of bears and bulls. Bulls have movements that project upward motion, and bears move project downward motion. Yes, I mean real bears in forests and bulls on farms.

With that in mind, bulls resemble buyers while bears resemble sellers in the financial markets. You will interact with terms like bearish and bullish candlesticks; remember the latter logic.

CHAPTER 1

What is a candlestick?

Financial Market is a broad term used to refer to a platform where securities are traded. These securities can be stocks, futures, derivatives, bonds, index funds, cryptos and more. In all these financial markets, technical analysis is not different. Market analysts and traders use the same systems, and candlestick charts are not exempted either.

You will realise that whether you want to use your technical analysis skills in the forex market or stocks market, you will have to understand candlesticks the same way any trader in the financial markets understands them. Traders tend to behave in similar patterns. Market drivers remain individuals and organisations creating supply and demand, thereby tossing the market up and down. Candlesticks do a great job of reflecting the behaviour of market participants in the most effective way.

CANDLESTICK PATTERNS FOR BEGINNERS

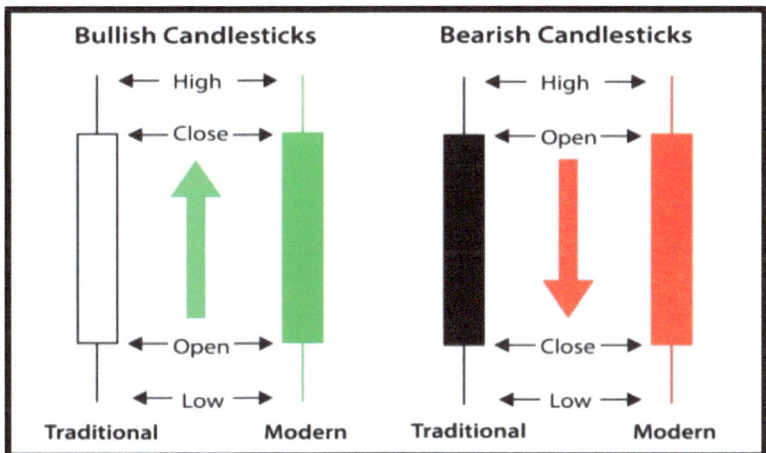

Candlesticks have two essential parts: the body and the wicks. The wick is the body's line extension, which shows prices reached by the market but were rejected. The body shows the net movement of the market from the time the market opened at a given period. The picture above shows two standard candlesticks; the green one is bullish and the red one bearish. The ends of the wicks are called highs and lows. The origin of the candlestick body is called the open, and the end of the body is also called the close.

The green candlesticks(bullish)

At the given time, the price started at the open; then it pushed down, reaching the low before pushing back past the open to form the body(*put your finger on the picture and follow the statement*). The body can only be created after moving past the candlestick's opening. The candlestick then pushes up to reach the price High before it retraces back and closes. The point at which the candlestick body stops for the time frame becomes its close similarly, where the body started is open. If the candlestick is a five-minute candlestick, then after five minutes, the candlestick closes. Whatever the price at which it closes becomes the close. After five minutes, a new candlestick opens at the same price as the previous close. Every price reached is not within the open, and the close of the candlestick is shown as a wick. The wicks show the high and the low of the candlestick.

However, the same logic can be applied to the bearish candlestick with the open at the top and the close at the bottom to exhibit downward movement.

You can note that candlesticks allow much information to be depicted in one picture.

Bullish movement

When the market starts to move up, the movement is called a bullish movement. It is dominated by green candlesticks, which are usually green(most if not all candlesticks will be green). Rarely there are instances of red (bearish candlesticks) due to the market experiencing slight jags called retracements. If you don't get it well, for now, it's okay. You will eventually understand, I'm sure.

Sometimes candlesticks in this movement have no wicks on top. That implies strong momentum to the upside, and the market is likely to continue manoeuvring in that direction long term.

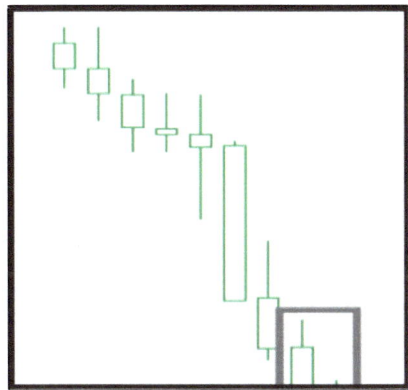

Bearish movement

A bearish movement is the opposite of a bullish move, with bearish candlesticks dominating the market. Unfortunately, the picture doesn't depict bearish candlesticks as red; instead, their bodies are white, which is also a ubiquitous chart presentation. This doesn't change what candlesticks mean (i.e. colour is not essential). However, green and red are almost the standard for most traders.

Note that there are instances where the candlesticks are enormous with no wicks. These represent periods of solid downward momentum, and the sellers are in control.

Now that you understand bullish and bearish movements, we can casually discuss candlestick patterns.

They are four candlestick patterns, and their consequences can be categorised into four groups. They are
- Bullish continuation patterns
- Bearish continuation patterns
- Bullish reversal patterns
- Bearish reversal patterns

CHAPTER 2

Bullish continuation patterns

From their names, you can discern what they are about. The bullish continuation pattern is a candlestick pattern found in a bullish trend or movement. Its role is to signify that the bullish moment still holds. When traders buy into a market, typically known as going long, they usually seek candlesticks with signals of a continuation of the movement. The overall activity forms a trend, i.e. a long trend(uptrend). Bullish candlesticks give them chances to add more to their long positions. That means they can buy more of the security or even enter fresh long positions on this security. I will put down samples of these candlestick patterns.

(To avoid the reality gap between textbook examples and real-life chart examples .l will use my chart pictures to explain these candlesticks.)

Doji Candlestick

The Doji candlestick is characterised by long wicks at the top and the bottom. The most important feature of this candlestick is its tiny candlestick body. The body is too small at times; the whole candlestick might look like a "+" sign in the market. In this case, the market was clearly in a bullish trend, and there was a minor pullback. There was a need for confirmation for a trend continuation.

As shown above, a Doji signalled the continuation of the trend. The market had been momentarily hijacked by bears(sellers); this could be because bulls were exiting their positions to profit; hence, bullish orders were reduced. The Doji depicts that since bears had gotten rid of bulls for the feel seconds, the bulls were getting in back for the tug of war. The long wicks notify traders that there is market indecision at the moment. As you can see, it also says no one is in control of the market. In a bullish trend, when the market gets temporarily neutral after bears try to push it down, it's only safe to bank on bulls as they have a previous record advantage. In this scenario, the Doji signifies the market is continuing to the upside. Now they are different variations of the Doji, but the logic is the same. It remains a sign of a fine balance in the market.

However, the long-legged ones might also bias the market drivers. For more variations, check out the picture below.

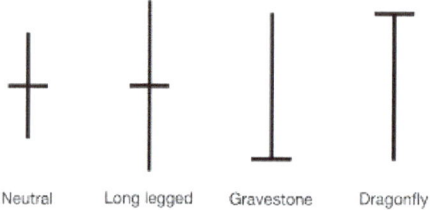

These are some of the Doji patterns worth knowing. Usually, the side with the longer wick denotes the one in control. For example, the dragonfly shows that bulls are in control. Always remember that wicks show abrupt price rejections to specific price points. Hence only strong market momentum can create wicks in a particular direction.

Doji can assess the short-term odds of the market continuing in the existing trend.

Three white Soldiers

This candlestick pattern is momentum-based. It is resembled by three clean green candlesticks(red for bearish movement) in a bullish move. By clean, there are no wicks on either side of the candlesticks. There is no tension in the direction; buyers are single-handedly driving the market and will most likely be in control for a while. The picture shows that there may be rejections and minor reversals, but the market direction remains upside as there is proof of strong buying power.

Other important momentum indicators can serve the same purpose. One of them is enormous candlesticks and market gaps. That implies that buyers (under uptrend conditions) firmly control the market and do not get enough liquidity at the gapped price levels.

The picture shows market gaps and giant candlesticks. You can see that the market continued with a long trend after these signs of momentum. When the market retraced to these regions of high momentum candlesticks, it pushed to the upside.

That occurs as a result of buyers gaining interest around these price levels. It is well known that buyers may decide to be very active at certain price levels and continually bet on them. Usually, these special prices of high interest are denoted by high momentum.

Hammer

A hammer is a typical candlestick with a long wick on either side and the bottom for bullish moves. Ideally, it looks like a literal hammer, the one you can buy in a hardware store. I bet there was no reason for me to say this as you had seen in yourself already.

We can see the hammer signals from the above picture that the bullish drivers will prevail. It is pertinent to know that the longer the wick, the stronger the odds of the expected movement. Sometimes the structure might not look like a typical hammer, but it is safe to say that whenever the wick is twice the length of the body, that's enough for it to be categorised as a hammer.

CANDLESTICK PATTERNS FOR BEGINNERS

Bullish Engulfing

A bullish engulfing pattern is when a bearish candlestick gets succeeded by a strong bullish candlestick, as shown. The simple logic behind this pattern is "buyers are a back inaction" more vital than ever after a slight loss in control. As a result, the market is expected to continue going up.

Bullish Harami

On this one, don't let the colours deceive you. The bullish harami typically has two candlesticks, with the first one being bigger, followed by a smaller candlestick, sometimes even opposite the market direction. However, they are unique; *the smaller candlestick has a way higher open than expected.* This creates an impression of a market gap; hence we go back to the concept of momentum again.

Tweezer bottom

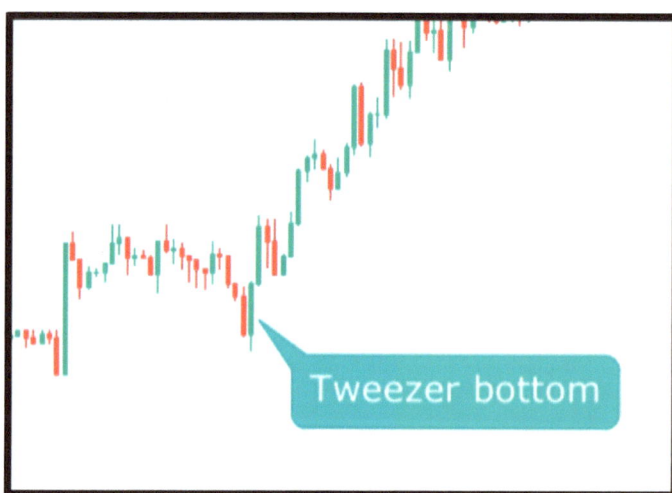

The tweezer bottom has ideally two equivalent in size opposite in direction candlesticks. In s bullish trend that is suffering a retracement, they show a continuation.

(Just a quick tip, the logic of the Doji applies here too. Think of it as a short-term balance between selling and buying power.)

When you see this candlestick and go to a twice as high time frame, you will see a Doji instead of a tweezer bottom. For instance, if you know a tweezer bottom in the 1HR time frame for the same time, this will be presented by a Doji on the 2HR time frame.

(If you find it easy to understand the logic behind these candlestick patterns, you are likely to find it easy to understand the ways for bearish moves as it is the same; however, using inverted thinking.NB: focus on the logic and not the names.)

CHAPTER 3

Bearish Continuation Patterns

Bearish continuation candlestick patterns are patterns that signal the continuation of a downtrend. They are very similar to bullish continuation patterns, except that these work in downtrends; I will try not to repeat many of the patterns and introduce new ones. You will realise the names are the same, usually with minor tweaks. The appearances are the same. The securities may take a short-lived upturn known as a correction in a downtrend. We look for bearish continuation patterns to ride the trend downside in this period.

Morubozou

Morubozou is a pure candlestick with no wick in both directions. This implies that it never suffered rejection when the market took the downside trajectory. Hence it explains the momentum direction as shown in the picture. The same candlestick can be found in a bullish setup and applies the same logic.

Bearish Engulfing

Undoubtedly, the Engulfing candlestick is the most represented candlestick pattern in any security. A giant bearish candlestick follows a bullish candlestick to signify downtrend movement in a bearish setup. Note that the bullish candlestick is at least below the neck level of the bearish candlestick in the picture. That reflects the momentum rules that we use in the market. Downward pressure will outweigh the upward force, and this could be a good sign that the market will continue going down.

Dragonfly Doji

This is a variation of the Doji candlesticks. Remember, a Doji candlestick shows equal market pressure in general. However, this one is biased as it has a long wick at the top. This implies the market has abruptly rejected higher prices in favour of the lower prices. This, in turn, notifies traders that the market is likely to turn down. Note that the same logic applies to the inverted hammer. Similarly, the inverted hammer has a long wick to the upside, almost twice as much as the body.

Tweezer tops

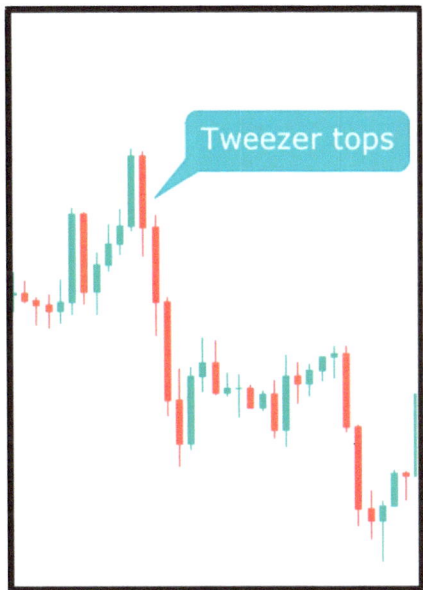

We have discussed tweezer bottoms in the previous section; similarly, we have tweezer tops in this section too. As shown in the picture, there are two equal but opposite candlesticks, with the bearish candlestick being the most recent one. This pattern's equal and opposite momentum is comparable to that of the "Doji" candlestick. As mentioned before, going to a twice-high timeframe for a tweezer top will give a Doji. (Always Remember that time frames are switched by combining candlestick patterns)

Dark Cloud Cover

This candlestick pattern comprises bullish candlesticks engulfed by two or smaller bearish candlesticks. Usually, the bearish candlestick starts slightly higher than expected. This may signify a gain in momentum to the downside.

CANDLESTICK PATTERNS FOR BEGINNERS

long Wicks

There are plenty more candlesticks, including clover and black crows; however, most candlestick patterns boil down to the structure of the wicks. Bearish continuation patterns have long wicks at the top side of the candlestick body. (Wicks signify strong rejection at certain price levels, and the longer, the more reliable they can be). We expect long wicks at the top for short(sell) trades in bearish setups.

CHAPTER 4

Trend Reversal Candlestick Patterns

In some securities, Trends regularly reverse, while in others, they don't. For example, the stock market and cryptocurrency markets tend to remain in one direction; on the other hand, in the forex market, trends change now and then. This is a generalisation. When trends reverse, the market charts leave signals and trails to show the possibility of an ultimate shift in direction. This includes candlestick patterns as well.

Please be advised not to solely use candlestick reversal patterns to execute reversal trades, as most patterns result in short-lived pullbacks. Using candlestick patterns with other technical or fundamental strategies pinpoints desired entries. As we discuss this section, you will realise that reversal patterns are not different from continuation patterns. However, these patterns show the complete end of the pre-existing trend and are usually well defined and robust.

Bullish reversal patterns

These patterns are seen at the end of a downtrend. The market will be starting to move upside. Most bullish continuation patterns apply in this section. However, l will focus on a few very significant ways that are very regular in most securities.

CANDLESTICK PATTERNS FOR BEGINNERS

The above shows Doji in different variations. Before reversal, various candlestick pattern combinations are exhibited for an extended period before the trend finally reverses. The patterns are similar to the ones discussed in the latter sections; however, they are in various combinations to show significant market rejection in this scenario. It is possible to see one rejection candlestick showing rejection too.

The picture shows a tweezer bottom single-handedly, signifying a shift in the trend. That is a rare situation as many repeated candlestick patterns present trend shifts in most cases. In this case, there is one strong tweezer bottoms pattern.

The appearance of these candlesticks remains pretty the same as the underlying effect is the same. In both cases, candlestick patterns result from a momentum shift in the financial markets.

Trend reversal can be signified by a series of long wicks opposing the pre-existing trend. In the above instance, the market was trending down. However, huge wicks are seen, each succeeding the previous one at a higher price. Eventually, the demand soars, proving that momentum has changed. The critical feature in this setup is the long wicks. The wicks form hammer candlestick patterns; however, the name isn't important at all. What's important is the direction of the wicks. Why wicks? As mentioned before, the wicks show opposing solid momentum. Who knows? That could be a significant sign of where the institutions are trading and their directions.

(Uses: You can use the above patterns to enter new long positions or short exit positions you are in.)

Bearish Reversal Candlestick Patterns

It wouldn't be fair to mention bullish reversal patterns and neglect bearish reversal patterns. However, the patterns have the same logic. I will use examples I did not say in the previous section to maintain novelty.

A strong bearish engulfing pattern can be seen before the market plunges. That is an apparent reversal from the previous uptrend. Note that a series of bearish engulfing succeeds this pattern to show continuation.

3 Black Crows

Like three white soldiers, the three black crows are a direct converse. It may signal the reversal of a trend. It is characterised by three bearish candlesticks and chart continuation patterns to confirm continuation patterns.

Uses: bearish reversal patterns can be used to take profit or exit long positions(buy). More so, it can be used to enter new short positions. That needs to be done in conjunction with other trading strategies. I will share some tips on implementing candlestick patterns in effective trading strategies.

Combination of candlestick patterns

If you double the time frame for the same market, you will get a different candlestick pattern; it is not essential to memorise names; instead, you should focus on the market movement presented. Time frames offer different candlestick patterns; however, the market movement depicted remains the same. Below are some examples of how candlestick patterns in a 1HR would appear in a 2HR timeframe.

1HR time frame_____ 2HR time frame

1HR time frame	2HR time frame
Tweezer bottom/ tops	Doji
Engulfing candlestick	One long wick candlestick
Three black crows	One long red candlestick and a red smaller candlestick (if the small candlestick doesn't combine with the next candlestick)

CHAPTER 5

How to trade with candlestick patterns

C andle stick patterns be a handy tool in trading. However, trading solely based on them could be a suicidal move. Hence every savvy trader has a solid trading strategy in which they implement their knowledge for candlesticks, primarily as confirmation of an already determined movement. I will focus on three common strategies that use candlestick patterns. Some methods may use EMAs(exponential moving averages) and Bollinger bands. However, I am pro price action so I won't include technical strategies and indicators. Don't take me for my word. Please feel free to try indicators; the logic remains the same. In other words, if you understand the underlying concept l am giving under this section, you can safely use the knowledge in any different strategy.

Trendline based strategy

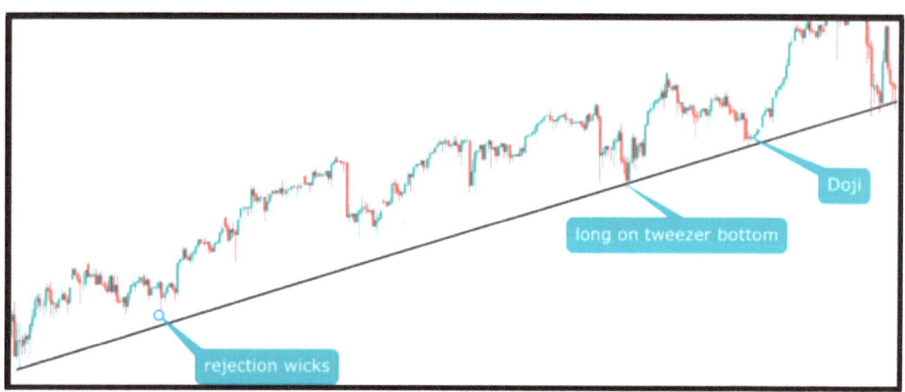

That is used by traders who focus on executing trades on their trend lines, whether short or long. They can concentrate on candlestick patterns formed when the market touches their trendlines. The above shows entry points for a long. The below picture shows entry points for short(sells). The same can be done using EMAs, SMAs, or Bollinger bands.

Trendline strategies are not reliable; they are traders who solely rely on their trendlines. I felt it would be vital for you to know what's out there. Generally, trendlines are essential in mapping out the market structure(the true price action series volume 2 market structure and technical analysis). You can take chances executing orders along with them.

Break and Retest based strategy strategies

Strategy is used for break and retest trading. I highly recommend this strategy, and I have elaborated it clearly in my other Ebook (*true price action series volume 4 to the advanced trader*). For now, I want you to focus on the precision of the short positions that could be taken on both entries 1 & 2. The beauty of candlestick patterns is that they give the trader the best prices to enter the market. In case of a short trade, they provide the highest prices to sell at.

Below is a setup for break and retest for long positions. Note the entries and the candlestick patterns on the entry points.

Demand and Supply strategy

This strategy focuses on finding institutional orders and trading along. This concept will be explained in detail in one of my later books (*the true price action series vol 3 supply and demand trading*). I highly recommend this trading strategy. However, at the moment, focus on the precision of the entries using candlestick patterns. If you already have a trading strategy, you might need to consider the entry points presented by candlestick patterns.

The above picture shows a demand level being retested(demand level in purple). Before the market reverses to soar, it exhibits a couple of rejection/reversal candlestick patterns. A seasoned trader would find entry points in the rejection area. The entry would be a five-star "sniper entry", as you can see from the chart above.

Below is a corresponding supply level being retested.

CANDLESTICK PATTERNS FOR BEGINNERS

The zoomed version of the picture shows the entry point that could be taken for a short in this market. The candlestick pattern shown is called tweezer tops. You can also see the precision of the entry. Generally, supply and demand are precise; however, knowing candlestick patterns would make the strategy more accurate and safer.

If you have read this section of the book, I believe you were eager to learn, and you have learned so much. Successful trading is a journey more than a destination. That implies you have to look out for more information and experience consistently.

(You might find checking out continuation for volumes 2 - 4 sound. Find them here on Amazon Best Wishes.)

SPECIAL ACKNOWLEDGEMENTS

I want to thank you for considering the write-up and the next ones. I also want to thank my family for supporting my work and encouraging me to put it out there to help others.

www.ingramcontent.com/pod-product-compliance
Lightning Source LLC
Chambersburg PA
CBHW040255220526
45473CB00001B/488